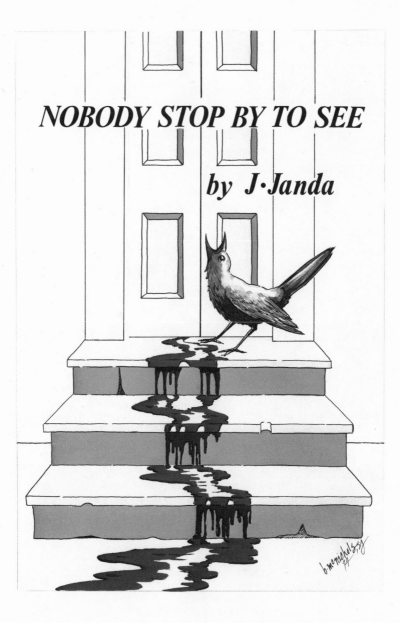

NOBODY STOP BY TO SEE

by J·Janda

NOBODY STOP BY TO SEE

POEMS
J. JANDA

PAULIST PRESS
New York/Ramsey/Toronto

Library of Congress
Catalog Card Number: 77-80807

ISBN: 0-8091-2040-2

Published by Paulist Press
Editorial Office: 1865 Broadway, N.Y., N.Y. 10023
Business Office: 545 Island Road, Ramsey, N.J. 07446

Printed and bound in the
United States of America

Contents

To
The North House Community
With
Love And Appreciation

Last September

WHILE the kids
was busting bottles
in the alley or

slinging cans at
passing trains

Granny was hollering
for them
to roll tires down the
street
or do something else

but Grandad wasn't
saying nothing

just sitting on the
porch watching sparrows
at the sunflowers or

staring in the
pokeberry bush growing
by the fence or

looking over his
last
patch of greens

Martha Washington

SHE got
   yellow newspapers
   covering her windows
   on the street side
   so nobody can look in
but she got a shade
   on the yard side one
   so she can see how
   the turnips   corn
   and beets is doing
and two police dogs
   to keep kids from
   stealing what she
   has planted 'cause
   she got to live
she make tea cakes for
   her church friends

East St. Louis

RAYETTA
with ashes in
her Afro
was forking over
ribs

there was this
uplifting wind

Kenyatta was
sweating
through his
dashiki

while
Granny was
letting Lester
know
in no uncertain
terms

that not-right
white child
was
going to taste
ribs and beans

in her yard
that night

or she'd be
upside
his thick head

Baby Soul

MAMA told
   Othella to hush
but Othella scream
   she had a
   roach
   in her stew
mama say
   it was rice
but Othella knew
   rice ain't got
   legs and feelers
   like roaches do

Preacher To Preacher

REVEREND Ames

after all the shouting
and hollering of
white dresses
dark with sweat ended

said that

fleeting things
like
rabbits in the collard
or hummingbirds in trumpet
creepers

helped him walk
through
forty-five years of
darkness
blacker than his skin

though
the Bible and preaching
got him started
and kept him on his feet
again and again

Mister R.R.

HE live
  in a brick house
  on a flat roof garage
  by the railroad yard
he keep
  a busted piano
  a washtub
  a office chair on wheels
  a broom and a
  barbecue grill
on his tarpaper porch
  which is the roof
his windows
  be clean
ever since
  I waved to him
from the viaduct
  on my way to work

Floyd Harris

HE lie
he cheat
he mean

when he
play cards

his old woman
say
he got a better
dis-
position in bed

Pop Bottles

THERE one there
  she say

he go behind the
  billboard
in the parking lot
  and come out
with a bottle
  stuck with leaves

the old folks
  be collecting
sody bottles
  and loading
them in their
  grocery cart

he wearing
  army pants
and a blue jacket
  showing red
and a baseball cap

she wearing
  a dress look like
old wallpaper
  with a pink sweater
when it turn cool

Back Yard

OLD mattress always
    damp from the rain

kids jumping on the
    bed springs

old police dog
    on his rusty chain
sniffing at the catfish
    smoking on the coals
    in the washtub
scratching at his fleas

petting him like
    scrubbing on a
washboard

he stop barking
    years ago
he know nobody gonna
    find anything
in this yard
    to sell for wine

Crazy Annie

She be walking
  and talking
all the time
  though no one
listening

somebody
  keep her in
pink sneakers
  white stockings
and a brown coat
  with a fur piece

and tie her hat
  under her chin

I pass her all the
  time but don't know
where she live

The Bridge

OH but the sky soft

like a pink and gray
    tiger kitten

evening coming on slow

everything else black
    like a ink drawing

        the high wire towers
        and lines
        with their easy hang

        the roofs
        tree tops and
        steeples

everything 'cept the
    silver railroad tracks
below me
    like long shiny snakes
sleeping early

        and the red glow of
            signal lights
        on the railroad bed

even the concrete bridge
  trembling from
the traffic
  like branches on a young tree

Pentecost For Sister Ozella

LAST night
   she couldn't sleep
kids was busting
   bottles and laughing
and shouting

she pray
   Lord ain't those
kids got nothing
   better to do

then a wind come
   rushing through
   her open windows
      drapes fly at her
      like the wings
      of a eagle
scattering newspapers
   all over the room

outside
   dead branches flying
   off the trees

   leaves spinning
   in the gutter

then the rain come
washing everything
   carrying the cellophane
   and cigarette butts
   down the street drain

when it stop
   everything clean
'cept for the broken glass
   gleaming in the street light

then she know

In The Vein

MAN   I mean
   I gots to stay
   in the crib
   all the time
them niggers
where I lives
is mean
   I makes it
   to the car
   and back
   but that the
   only scene

        what you want   boy

        I got me a tool shed
        'cept ain't no tools in it
        I got me a arsenal

        what you need   man

        a derringer
        a automatic
        something big
        something small

        cat got to have
        a little protection
        these days and

ain't nobody
gonna know
'cept you and me

man
   nobody gonna mess
   with me now
don't have to buy
   this dog no chow
it fit right here
   in my pocket
nice and lean
   this dude doing
the town
   making the scenes

ain't afraid talking
   to nobody now
'cept that cat
   who shoot
wine in the vein

Mo Lester

FIRST he let his conk
   grow out and buy
hisself a pic for his 'fro

then he cut down his 'fro
but don't tell why
   say he tired
   explaining things
even when the brothers
   say he
      Uncle Tommin' it

only his folks ain't asking
   questions
even when everybody say he
   think he
      Black Jesus

You Dig

I been
watching this sister
you dig

she got
this big 'fro
and two
other big things
you dig

one day
I finds her alone
you dig

suddenly
we soul to soul
you dig

she say
brother   you really
serious 'bout the movement
you dig

she pull off her 'fro
she bald as her sisters
in Nigeria   you dig

she look at me and scream
OCOMOGOSIAY   you dig

From The High-Rise

SOME be
  behind buildings
  in the alley

some be
  in store-front
  assemblies

some be
  dancing and carrying on
  in local candy shops

always gathering 'round
something with somebody

Boone's Farm wines

the Jackson Five

or 'round someone
  who claim he been
up the mountain

man got to
  gather 'round something
to make it

The Visit

THE Crib of Bethlehem
plant
put out those long arms

the end curl up just like your
hand
and the bloom look just like
the
Christ Child in the crib

oh it smell so good
the smell go to
the other room
in the house and the

flowers is so pretty
it's a shame
nobody stop by to see

Toward A Definition

To have
  swallowed smoke
and shared bread
  with roaches

to have lived in a
  new house
with shattered windows
  and moved back

yet keep something
  green
in old windows

  is to be Black

Lord

Can't even run across
the street
these days without
a police car
slowing down to a stop

can't even smile at a
stranger
without him thinking you
gay
or trying to unload some
grass
or out for some ass

can't even spend a
afternoon
in a coffee shop
wondering
    why people who never
    come out
    of their hives
    throw
    crumbs out the window
    for sparrows
if you don't drink
at least
two quarts of coffee

guess that's
why
I so black

Look Man

I just got back from
Vietnam
want to see the scar on
my leg

don't go puttin' your
hand
in your pocket

I don't want no more
fightin'
see the scar on my
neck

the truth is
see them chicks over there
I got to have me
some pussie

now five dollars
gonna put
gas in the tank

see that Falstaff sign

in a hour
you go in and ask
for Jenkins

the cat who popped
a hundred
last night
and you got your
money back

Jack

Yeh

THEY know
  he a loud talkin'
  big black mother fuckin'
  honky hatin' nigger
who jive on the Panther line

he really black
with strong white teeth
he a African chief

once he put a arm lock
on a tea colored cat—
made him squeal like a
hog caught under a fence

he make the white boys cringe
and the white girls drool

his girl don't cringe
his girl don't drool
she got more sense

she know
  he got a gardenia
blooming inside
  and if she just
touch it
  it gonna shrivel up
and die

Home Town

FREIGHT cars
loaded with coal

hazed with snow

piles of ties

sheds in the
railroad yard

down the street
windows of brick factories
reflect
windows of brick factories
across the street

steam dribbling down
windows of a cafe

blurred peoples
hunching over the counter
and juke box

tin newsstand
filled with
dead leaves
paper cups
knotted twine

dead pigeon
rolling across the sidewalk
in the wind

barbed wire gone up too

Revolution

A memory

passed on

then written down

a 2,000 year old best seller

millions of copies

a story told

from mouth to mouth

then printed

still hot on the press

in almost every language

*   *   *

a memory

a story told

passed on

from mouth to mouth

then written down

then printed

a 2,000 year old best seller

a strange woman

a mysterious child

she could not understand
but tried to

lived and was killed

for claiming to be God

the story has it

he reappeared to his friends
after his death

still hot on the press

millions of copies

in almost every language

cooked them fish

and much to their chagrin
said he'd leave them

but at some future time
would come back again

                 *   *   *

he made another promise

a promise he kept

a promise to put the
   Promise
in each man's heart

one they'd live to see

so the story says

a real promise
a living promise
a breathing promise

a promise he called
   the Holy Spirit
he would live
   in the heart

he say

the Holy Spirit
in everybody
if you believe

if you got the Promise
people say you drunk

but
   you got to believe

you got to trust
you got to feel his Promise

                if you listen
                you'll know

something inside telling you
   you good
   you something special
   you worth it

                your body good
                your mind good
                your soul good

you is good

                you is full of Promise

you got to keep that Promise
you got to hold that Promise
you got to care for that Promise
   like a little bird in your hand
   like a flame of a candle
     don't let it go out
   like a flower blooming in the snow

                *   *   *

a memory

                her name Mary

a story told

                he born in a crib

passed on

                she could not understand
                her son
                but tried to

then written down

                the establishment
                was out to get him

then printed

                for claiming to be God

a 2,000 year old best seller

the story has it

on the night before he died

before his friends left him
before the police got to him

before they'd beat him
before they'd spit on him
before they made a fool
    out of him

before his unjust trial
before his sentence
before his execution

he took some bread

it was a party

he broke up the bread

they had wine and sang

he gave them bread

all his friends
were around him
at the table

he say

do this in memory of me

don't let me die in your minds
don't let me die in your hearts

don't let me die

remember me

            *   *   *
a memory

he say

I will be with you always

a story told

33

passed on

from mouth to mouth

then written down

then printed

a 2,000 year old best seller

I will not leave you orphans

little children
do not be afraid

I am sending you
the Promise

he will heal you
he will comfort you

in your hearts
he will tell you
what to say

do not be afraid

remember me

*   *   *

Due To Recent Holdups
We Can Admit
Only Those We Know

THE kids

being
closer to the
ground

seen them

the old folks seen
them
they always looking
down

Odell seen them
when
he was shot down

talking about
dandelions
at the fence
by the
food store

If You Don't Have Nothing To Do Don't Do It Here

M~AMA~ ask
   you flunk another
   subject in school

daddy ask
   boy when you gonna
   find yourself a job

sister ask
   when you gonna stop
   being so nasty with me

grandma say
   you getting a little
   thin and nervous lately

Grocery Shopping

SOMETIME

the load
get
so heavy

I gots
to rest

and so
I sits on the
park bench

and sees
how tall and strong
the trees is

and recollects
what
Paul say

I can do all things
in Him
who strengthen me

then walks

again

Mama Got To Work

SOMETHING silencing songs
when songs should come

something freezing joints
when dancing should be done

something stopping up words
locking up the tongue

some stinking bad yeast
growing in our young

Grandma Say

AIN'T nobody
gonna hurt you
like

    your mama got to
    run out of breath
    sometime

    and the police
    stops chasing
    when you stops
    loitering at
    that food store

    nobody keeping
    records on you
    'cept at school

ain't nobody
hurting you
like
you hurting
yourself baby

now what was you
saying
about my cinnamon
apples

how could I
forget
them raisins

Soulard's Before Christmas

A smoggy goose
with orange feet
and orange rings
around his eyes

was looking at me
from behind the bars
of his wooden cage

there was piles of
    white onions
    red onions
    green onions
oranges and limes

sacks of walnuts
    hickory nuts
    chestnuts
pecans and peanuts

there was
    mustard greens
    collard greens
    beet greens
heaps of greens
    greener greens
    I ever seen
or heard of

there was
   fish for your belly
   fish for your tank
catfish   sunfish
staring on ice
   guppies and goldfish
a puppy rolling over
chewing at his lice

there was
   cages of cats
   cages of rats
guinea pigs   dogs
turtles for sale

cages of rabbits
   white rabbits
   black rabbits
   brown rabbits

black and white rabbits
brown and white rabbits
black brown and white rabbits

and Nadeen in her
   new boots and blown 'fro
   was saying
buy me that integrated bunny

honey

Homicide

OLD Sadie
walking
crazy Joe

to the show
and back

and feeding
him
for nothing

once made
the mistake
of telling him

she love him

he didn't talk
much
after that

but one day
he shot her

Lullaby

Baby   baby
brown sugar child
mama never gonna leave you
close your eyes
close your eyes

   daddy gone north
   looking for a job
   Jason gone out to play
   granny cooking at
   that church fry
   soon it will be day

baby   baby
brown sugar child
mama never gonna leave you
close your eyes
close your eyes

   landlord giving 'nother
   month for rent
   welfare check coming tomorrow
   who need gas heat
   in spring
   church gonna let us borrow

baby   baby
brown sugar child

mama never gonna leave you
close your eyes
close your eyes

   granny hold you
   in the day time
   mama hold you at night
   daddy coming back
   some morning
   everything gonna be alright

baby   baby
brown sugar child
mama never gonna leave you
close your eyes
close your eyes

Black Sheep

SISTER-in law

come in
on the Greyhound
all cut up

before

it was only
black eyes
and bruises

or

a empty pocketbook

this time
daddy loose his cool
say
one more time Reginald
do it

he gonna visit
Alabama
and when he finish
won't be
much of Reginald
left

Brother

IF you down
if you worried
if you low

get off your dead ass
do something
for some white mother

buy him a can of
Afro-Sheen

offer him your pic

ask him would he like
some grits

even if you don't
understand
it's part of my plan

this is the
Lord talking

zap

My Beloved

HE was so kind
before
he start drinking

she keep telling
everybody
all the time

yet everybody know

her mother-in-law
her family and friends
her preacher

even her kids
understand

you got to shoot
when
somebody coming
at you
with a butcher knife
in hand

Welfare

W HITE lady
with a baby
and a box

come in the store

asking
could she be
refunded
on the Christmas cards
she bought

say her husband
didn't like that
kind and could
she look at some
more

she left with
the refund

Local Clergyman Suspected Of Rape

Y EH girl

it's a shame

them mens
won't
listen to him
no more

not that they
any better

and his mama

feel so bad
when
she see his
picture
in the paper

everybody complaining
he say one thing
and do another

peoples is mean

he never claim he Jesus

Country Boy

WHO say the city
so bad
same stuff growing
wild here

morning glories is
on the fence

pokeberries growing
along side the
busted refrigerators

sunflowers blooming
out of
that wreck convertible

cornflowers and old tires

even got
grasshoppers jumping
on the
car hoods

watch out for the glass
sugar

I loves living
'cause it's July

and hot
and pulling down
sweaty heads
is my business
baby

and this here junk yard
is good a place as any

Slowing Up Traffic

Yes they be
  playing jump rope
and baseball
  and roller skating

in the middle
of the street

officer
  can nobody stop
them
  from having fun

even after
  they see my Willie
here run down
  besides   where else

they got to play
  kids is kids

Talking To A Wall

FREDDIE May
catch
her old man
fooling
with that young
girl
    again
she didn't say
nothing
this time
    but
when he come
home
she busted his
fifth
and use it on his
face
    can
hardly recognize
him
no more

Redevelopment

YOUR grandaddy

never did
get it together
son

but

when the
house
was still there
we used
to sit on the
stoop

and look
and look
and look

until
your daddy
come by

he'd
hold you and
look
and look
and

let's you and
me carry some
Tasty Freeze
back to granny

Elevators

OTIS elevator man
say
he can't think up
nothing
the kids couldn't work out

even
after my girl here got
raped
and Mrs. Higgins here got her
jaw
broke and her purse grabbed

by
some young dudes we
ain't
never seen before which
ain't
saying nothing new 'cause

is
more kids here than
monkeys
at the zoo though them
animals
is much better off

seeing they all got protection

Inadequate Housing

MAY look like
Dresden

     baby

but slums
is where
the action

      is

and nobody
gonna look
for you here

     even

though you
own
much of this
place

    and

what I'm selling
ain't gonna ruin
your enterprise

you want the
down payment
now or later

High-Rise

JAMES here was born
in the hall
couldn't get the elevator
that day

'course kids use them
for toilets
who can hold out from one
to nine

firemens got bricked
last week
when they tried putting out
a trash fire

no police coming around
this place
black or white   red
or yellow

this white chief tell me
sixty per cent
of the crime 'round here
done around

the elevators and the only
thing we safe

from is the Mafia
I wonders

what their going price is

Night Shift

GRANNY had a nicked
earthenware jar

brown on the outside
white on the inside

she used to take off
the shelf and with a

eggbeater mix me a
cold chocolate milk

when I couldn't sleep
and mama wasn't around

and watch me drink and
say little things
like this   saves a day

Matricide

IT was
your mama this
and
your mama that
like
we always be
saying
to each other

didn't
know it was true
in
Ronnie's case

and
that her business
put
bread and beans
on
the table

she
was so pretty
in
the coffin
just
like a angel

though
Ronnie
never did see
being
behind bars

Layed Off

I was wearing
torn tennis shoes
ripped levi's
and a pea jacket

he was wearing
the shoulderless
top coat with
a greased collar

this time he
look at me

see it his
turn to give

so he smile

Her Daddy Big And Mean

I approaches the phone

dials

waits

it's ringing

the receiver go up

all is still

I hears someone breathing

ah, er, is Pat home

then this big voice
comes booming over

WHO DO YOU WANT
WHO IS THIS

I say

sorry

guess I got the
wrong number

SIR

Anthropology

I means
culture is how
you be raised
Jack

have nothing to
do with the color
of your skin

like if you was
raised by Eskimos

you'd be eating
seal and whale
'stead of
neck bone and grits
hocks and beans

and you'd have
a bad time
messing with them
sisters
in all that fur

Broken Window: Lloyd And Floyd

You did
you did
you did

sucker
sucker
sucker

you lie
you lie

mama gonna find out

I don't know about you

you retarded

ain't no use talking

mama   Floyd did it

here come mama

ouch   no   he did it

damn

you had it coming

nigger

you did
you did
you did

sucker
sucker
sucker

you lie
you lie

mama gonna find out

I don't know about you

you retarded

ain't no use talking

mama   Lloyd did it

here come mama

ouch   no   he did it

damn

you had it coming

nigger

Retired

THEY be laughing
at him
everytime he come out
of the house

since he trim
the hedge
to the ground
for her

so she
keep him inside most of
the time now

every night
she wash the dishes and
he dry
and when they is done

she put
them away wet
knowing

a man got
to work to keep
his pride

After School

KIDS using
broomsticks for
baseball bats

'cause

bats get stolen
quick
and crying ain't gonna
help

'specially when
broomsticks is
around in
every back yard

and there always
be
somebody who
interested
in
unofficial fun

Spring Nights

EVERYBODY be sleeping
when I gets home from
the grill

but I picks up my
sleeping child and
plays with

him and carries him
to the back porch and
sits and

sings to him till he
fall asleep   I falls
asleep

some time too watching
the branches move on
the tree

or the lady across the
alley walking in her
kitchen or

listening to clicking
of dog feet on the
side walk

and the tinkling of glass
he has stepped on without
hurting

his feet   they say priests
be up praying at this
hour too

The Daughters Jefferson

Y ELLOW coat
pink coat
baby blue coat

lavender dress
mint green dress
fuchsia dress

each with matching
socks
and oh so white
shoes
(patent leather)
and
shiny white purses

and avocado, white,
peach, and lime
green bows on the
patch braided heads

they rolled out of
the Cadillac
like eggs out of a
Easter basket
into the Church of the
Pre-Sanctified

'cause daddy got paid
and everyone know
you got to go to church
on Sunday 'specially
when they celebrating
the Lord's Resurrection

Moving On Up

T HE high-rise be
equipped
with everything

but
he go and sell
his
facilities at
night

like
I means his toilet
his
sink and electric
fixtures

and
be buying hisself
wine

'cause
it the only thing which
help
him face a new
day

since
he come home from
work

to find his child half
eaten

by rats

and his wife carrying on
like a baby

Sister Carrie Of The Church
Of Christ The Divine

Sister-in-law
done got dropsy

brother in jail
for taking dope

rheumatism
in my joints
but I gots
to stand at
this grill
all day

but don't you
worry brother
you'll get well

even if you
can't tell me
what it is

when we witnesses
we gets strength

your load help
me lift mine

this coffee I made
sure taste good
if I do say so myself

Baptism

W<small>ATER</small>

shooting out
the hydrant

water

kids
jumping in it
dancing in it
splashing in it

water

flooding the street
stopping up traffic
cooling
off the feet

water

kids running in it
kids yelling in it
kids laughing in it

water

grandad holding
junior Joe
in diapers in it
so he can
kick with his feet

water

reminding us
we sons of God
and
can no ordinance
deny
us the joy

if it do
stones and bricks
gonna shout out
the truth

Independence Day

THOMAS Jefferson
with a big blue
umbrella
yellow short pants
white shoes
and a pink shirt

was looking up
in the back of a
truck
at striped
watermelons piled
high
in straw

'cause it be
the Fourth of July
and mama
being home from work
was wanting
something special
to go
with her ribs and
beans

which is
pleasantly smoking

in hickory chips
on the grill
on the back porch

it had to rain
she keep saying
it had to rain

but

the kids watching
TV
and dancing on the
front porch
and chasing each other
'round the
house with plastic
umbrellas

don't mind
'cause
they been celebrating
the Fourth
for the past month
with
sparklers   rockets
cherry bombs
and super snappers

providing
the old folks with
something
to talk about
when

they gets up
like
saying how they
couldn't
sleep till two AM
and
why don't some
families
mind their offsprings
better

nerve pills be
relaxing
the body but don't
put
the mind to rest
though
they has to admit

firecrackers
be
better to fool with
than
gasoline and kerosene
bombs

which
some kids getting
into
for some new kind of

revolution

Cockles In The Wheat

GOSPEL music coming
through
open windows

leaves barely moving
on the sycamore tree

two kids playing cards
on the steps of the laundry
dog at their feet

sun making laces
in the halls
shining through
the leaves

sunflowers and chicory
bringing
the sun and heaven
down
to earth

sparrow making a big
fuss
in the tree 'cause the
cat
looking through the screen
eyeing
her offspring

Sunday morning
calm and bright
like the seventh
day of creation

enjoy it brother

when the sun go down
some gonna be using
ice picks, guns, and
razors like Cain did

spoiling things for
the rest of mankind

A Sower Went Out To Sow

Seeds

planted
in the earth
planted
in the dark

seeds

when watered
will grow

seeds

sending out roots
pushing up the earth

seeds

reaching
for the sun
waiting
on the rain

seeds

rooting in me
growing in me
stretching in me

oaks and elms
rising up
out of my feet

grapes and wheat
bearing fruit
out of my hands

bleeding hearts
blooming
out of my side

violets and bluebells
flowering
out of my ears

grass waving
on my head

no more wind
can
blow me away

Blood

Blood
on the door posts
blood
on the doors

blood
running through the
ghetto

human blood
running
down the sewers

Lord
I know no tomb
could hold you
but

how long
bleeding Jesus
you
gonna bleed

bleeding Jesus
how long you
gonna hang there

bleeding Jesus
ain't nobody
gonna take you down

brothers and sisters
sons and daughters
all my black children

who you be beating
who you be blinding
who you be slaying

they be Jesus you
beating
they be Jesus you
blinding
they be Jesus you
slaying

they be Jesus
'cept
you never gonna
see
them rise from the
tomb

only bleed

Double Funeral

YOUR young wife
and child
be taken from you
son

they was given
to you
for a short time
to let
you know that
love be

listen
the Lord trying
to tell
you something

he saying
Clyde
everybody
in life or death
belongs
to me

it is I
who makes you
happy

and I has some
surprises for you
up my sleeve

Mystical Rose

STOP talking
'bout color

white black brown
red or yellow

if you prays
you be all God-colored
which is to say

you be bathed
in the essence of God
who possess

all color

you flow into Him
He flow into you

you gonna forget
distinctions
they never did help

but only if you willing
to put up with
a little darkness and pain

Randy's Mama

LORD
yes he stole and
killed

sold junk
got kids hooked
and

this
here child be his
son

but he done it for me

'cause
I can't do no
work

with
this aching in my
bones

when
I touches his face behind
bars

I cries

Jesus
be under that
'fro

and he got to suffer

Skeeter's Farm

DEER tracks
still running to the
mud pond

coon tracks
there too

old wood chuck
lumbering
across the road

got some spit-bug
mess
on my jeans gathering
Queen Ann's lace
tiger lilies
and milkweed
for granny's kitchen

she say
all that wild onion
in the field
ruining
the cow's milk

and
sent me to the white
folks

for some heavy cream
so
she could whip me up
some
real ice cream
and
make my vacation complete

Blackberry Picking

AIN'T you
happy you wearing
Gator's
shirt and jeans
child

this briar
can scratch
and prick

just pick
the black ones
baby
when they red
they ain't
ripe

after
your child come
raise
it right here with
me

ain't no use
messing up
God life in
that city

Employment Office

FIRST

the wife
was sick

then

the kids
was sick

I had to
take off
for them

then

my mother-in-law
decided
to try dying

I figured
the job would wait
but
she wouldn't

I guess
that ain't so
'cause she alive

and I is applying
for something new

Deacon Dorcas

THEY was
cattails and
water lilies
by the river

chicory and
butterfly weed
on the roadside

partridge peas too

which is saying
nothing
of all them trees
sassafras
osage orange
and magnolia

and fields of wild
flowers
white   pink   blue

all the colors
of the rainbow

in the city
you learns
what mens make

in the country
you witnesses
what God make

he sure do
know
how to paint
and
design

Dependable Maid

LIGHTNING
hit that oak
and tore it
wide open

never would
have guessed
it was
rotted out
inside

and Lord
Mr. Williams
after the last
of his kids
got married

shot hisself

he always
stood
so tall

Trees

I feels guilty
stepping
off the bus

it be dim and
cool
like a cathedral
walking
down the boulevard
of trees
to my housekeeping

there be sun
spots
on long lawns
and
birds singing

nothing like

only bricks
asphalt
and concrete

which hold
heat
but the city

don't plant
trees
where I lives

and the only place for
my kids
to play is the streets

Seeing They Don't See

SHE be waving
that
red and white
cane
like conducting
a
orchestra

turning and swaying
at
the same time

holding that tin
cup
in the other hand
on
Olive and Grand

honey, who say you
got
to be blind to beg

most folks avoiding
what
they can't understand

Homecoming

MY college trained
brother-
in-law just
got
back from Nigeria

let me tell
you
that dude un-
happy

couldn't talk
their
language

got sick
on
native cooking

and he say
is
more bugs
there
than he seen
in
biology books

screaming
night birds wasn't
so bad

but
a snake on his
bed
put him on the
next

jet

home

Eulogy

YOU put your
foot
on it   she

did have
quite
a appetite

mens was like
flowers
to her and she

picked them all

except one
she never
did say much
about

I can't judge
her
no sir, not
me

she always be
buying clothes
for my kids

who else
besides God
be perfect

August

WHITE hot sun
reflecting
off the pavements
and bleached
board fences

black ladies
in white dresses
sitting
on card table chairs
against
whitewashed bricks

fanning themselves
with newspapers

talking and watching
among other things

the big white smoke
coming off
the barbecuing ribs

'cross the street
weeds
be high as the heaps of
tin cans
exhaust pipes and
car frames

but on the
hot rusting fence
light
coming through blue
morning glories
like
church windows

Thanksgiving Dinner

THAT'S true

my home
burned
right to the
ground

just when

Mr. Murray
my deceased
was
ready to enjoy
his pension

but

no chance
about it

I believes
that fire
be
for a
purpose

we here
for
a purpose

as I said
before
no chance
about it

everything
happen for a
purpose

Cornered

Baby don't
not in front of
the kids

my sister in
Alabama
gonna come through
I know
she will

and why you
too proud
for welfare

you bring one
more man
in my house

gonna be
one less nigger
in this city

that's right

soon as he
come through
that door

you'll find out

Zoning

I hears hammers
pounding
nails in wood

and
sees mens fencing
over
windows of the lady's
house
'cross the street

she
being up in her years
finally
got together enough
for
her and her husband
to
buy the house

ain't
nothing much
but
some dudes
broke
in and took her
TV
last week

which
really ain't saying
much

'cause
jobs is scarce
and
TV ain't a
matter
of life and death

but
this neighborhood
getting
to look like a
concentration camp
with all that
fencing up

'cept the government
ain't footing the bill

Don't Turn In The Collar

REVEREND

I satisfies mens'
short term needs

you has got to
satisfy some long
range plans

so keep smiling
both
of us be mentioned
in
the Bible

and I quitting
this
profession
soon
as my mortgage
paid

The Question

WHY go to the
moon
to look around

plenty to see
around here

maybe it ain't
that pretty
but it could be

NASA may benefit
some
in the long run

but

so many peoples
on earth
be happy to see
some trees

and a little
national
interest
in the
neighborhoods

then

folks
wouldn't have to
drive
to the suburbs on
Sundays
to see trees

Our Father

A child be shot
on
the playground

who art in heaven

a teenager shot
in
the throat
in
a study hall
for
not handing
over
his coat

hallowed be thy name

a pregnant woman
kicked
in the stomach
her
kids beat up

thy kingdom come

oh let it come
oh let it come

'cause
Our Father
you ain't in heaven
Our Father
you in our hearts
Our Father
if you any place
you in us

but
Our Father
you losing your
kingdom

Our Father
you losing your
crown

you gotta let us
    carry knives
you gotta let us
    carry guns
you gotta let us
    carry clubs

ain't never been a
kingdom
on this earth
built
with love

gonna take bullets
to let you in some
heads

gonna take bullets

to let you in some
hearts

but
then it would be
too
late, Our Father
too
late, wouldn't it

Our Father

Job Daniels

GRANDAD

found
his older brother
shot
in the bathtub

and

heard
his younger brother
hung
hisself in a clothes
closet

these things
being
told us by
mama
his daughter

who'd
never let us kids
mess
with grandad
while
he was feeding
squirrels

'cause she say

squirrels
and
cornflowers
took
the place of
them

for him

Etta

NEVER would
give up
that retarded
child

she took it with
herself
wherever she went

and she could
smile
and take it by the
hand
when other kids
was
mean to it

some kind of
understanding
we couldn't get

though

every year she
walked a little
more bent

after it
died
she passed

I believes
she
accomplished
that
for which
she
was sent

Police Gun Down Youth

Not saying much
was
     mama

but the closed
Bible
     and

letting her hair
go
     started

worrying us
till
     the day

she asked Rodney
to
     fetch

her Annie Mae's
curtain

     stretcher

City Hospital

YOU deacons
be
so good to
me
and the family

she said

tell me
if you please
when I
be in that coma
did nobody
stop by to see

no
Talitha
I said

nobody stop by to see

Front Room Window

IN her room
in the window
be
two planks
loaded with
plants
and empty jars

for one hour
each day the
sun
shines on the
plants and
fills
the jars with

light   they catches
the light and holds
it
I can see you
notices   what is
empty
can be filled

City Jail

SHE sat there with
dignity
she was composed
almost
like a judge so
sure
he's got to be
there
everything depends on
him

which son was it this
time
or was it a grandson

she knew and would
tell
if questioned
for
she had nothing to
hide
nothing to prove

caring had taught her
to
be there   caring and the
call

to be a mother
no
matter who the father was

all of which she
admitted
came through prayer

Wedding Plans

SHE
did get the courage
to

ask
for a loan
for

the
rings and refreshments
'cause

old
friends and some
new

would
be there to see
the

beginnings
of something she
knew

would
last a long
time

Holy Saturday

SHIRTS and pants
jumping
on the loose line
drying
in the wind rushing
blowing
'round the back

porch

which provide a
view
of the sky and a
patch
of grass to tell
that
seasons pass

confirming

what is felt
in the bones

Blighted Area

THE mortgage be
almost
paid on this old
house
full of roaches

but I got my
own
bedroom in the
attic

and though a black-
bird
get in and scare
me
half to death

I can look out
my
window and see the
red
brick alley

and robins and a
squirrel
making her nest in a
hole
in the walnut tree

in the front
yard
be a rosebush the
white
family planted

years ago

and in the back
when
I carries out the
trash

I finds violets
blooming
in the weeds